COUNTRIES OF THE WORLD

AUSTRALIA

ROBERT PROSSER

Evans

TITLES IN THE COUNTRIES OF THE WORLD SERIES:
AUSTRALIA • BRAZIL • CHINA • EGYPT • FRANCE • GERMANY
ITALY • JAPAN • KENYA • MEXICO • UNITED KINGDOM • USA

Published by Evans Brothers Limited
2A Portman Mansions
Chiltern Street
London W1U 6NR

Produced for Evans Brothers Limited by
Monkey Puzzle Media Limited
Gissing's Farm, Fressingfield
Suffolk IP21 5SH, UK

VISIT OUR WEBSITE
Evans
www.evansbooks.co.uk

First published 2004
© copyright Evans Brothers 2004

British Library Cataloguing in Publication Data
Prosser, Robert
Australia. – (Countries of the world)
1.Australia – Juvenile literature
I. Title
994

ISBN 0 237 52618 2

Editor: Susie Brooks
Designer: Jane Hawkins
Map artwork by Peter Bull
Charts and graph artwork by Encompass Graphics Ltd
All photographs are by Bill Bachman, except *ANT Photo Library* 15 (Gordon Claridge), 33 bottom (Bill Bachman), 52 top (Jack Cameron), 56 (Nick Tonks), 57 (Natural Images); *Corbis Digital Stock* front and back endpapers; *Holden Ltd* 46; *Mike Langford* 43 top; *Port Waratah Coal Services, Newcastle* 48 bottom; *Bill Sampson* 17 top right; *Wildlight Photo Agency* 37 top (Philip Quirk).

Endpapers (front): Sydney Opera House and business district, seen from across the harbour.
Title page: Mustering sheep in the Outback.
Imprint and Contents page: A farm on the Stirling plains in Western Australia's wheat belt.
Endpapers (back): Uluru (Ayers Rock).

CONTENTS

The Australian flag is made
up of the Union Jack (top left),
the Star of Federation (bottom
left) and the stars of the
Southern Cross constellation.

INTRODUCING AUSTRALIA

Australia is a land of glorious coastlines and other spectacular scenery.

Australia is the sixth-largest country in the world and the second-largest island (after Greenland). Because of its immense size and isolation, it is also considered a continent in itself. Australia lies in the Oceania region of the southern hemisphere, between the Indian and South Pacific Oceans. It consists of a vast main island, plus Tasmania – a small island state to the south-east – and several tiny coastal islands.

Compared to most countries, Australia has a short political history. European settlers claimed the land in 1788, and for more than 100 years it was divided into separate British colonies. It was not until 1901 that six of these colonies joined together as a federation of states (Queensland, New South Wales, Victoria, Tasmania, South Australia and Western Australia). In 1911, two final territories joined (Northern Territory and Canberra, Australian Capital Territory).

INDONESIA

PAPUA NEW GUINEA

— Main roads
---- Railways
✈ International airports

N

Darwin ✈

INDIAN OCEAN

Gulf of Carpentaria

Great Barrier Reef

SOUTH PACIFIC OCEAN

NORTHERN TERRITORY

Cairns ✈

QUEENSLAND

Tropic of Capricorn

Uluru (Ayers Rock)

Alice Springs

WESTERN AUSTRALIA

SOUTH AUSTRALIA

Lake Eyre

Brisbane ✈

Lake Everard
Lake Gairdner

Lake Torrens

NEW SOUTH WALES

Perth ✈

Great Australian Bight

Adelaide

Canberra

Sydney ✈

AUSTRALIAN CAPITAL TERRITORY

VICTORIA

Melbourne ✈

SOUTHERN OCEAN

Tasman Sea

0   500   1000km
0   600 miles

TASMANIA

Hobart ✈

THE COMMONWEALTH

Each of Australia's states has its own parliament and its own identity, but the central, federal government is based in the nation's capital, Canberra. The federal system is known formally as the Commonwealth of Australia, and when Australians refer to 'the Commonwealth' they usually mean their own country and government. This can be confusing as Australia, having once been a colony, is still a member of the British Commonwealth. Although Australia is an independent country, the British queen is legally the Head of State, with a Governor General acting as her representative. It is likely that in the future this link with the UK will be broken and Australia will become a republic.

ABORIGINAL ORIGINS

Although British settlers did not arrive until the eighteenth century, Australia's cultural history extends much further back in time. The first inhabitants were the Aborigines, who migrated there from South-east Asia at least 50,000 years ago. In 1788 there were approximately 300,000 Aborigines, scattered across the country in semi-nomadic groups. Today many Aborigines remain, though their lifestyles have largely changed.

Balloons float over Canberra on Canberra Day, a yearly festival marking the city's birthday.

PACIFIC LINKS

Australia retains close ties with the UK, but its economic and political future lies increasingly across the Pacific world. This stretches from the USA to the expanding economies of East and South-east Asia. Australia has made a number of trade, military and security pacts within this broad region, often in partnership with its neighbour New Zealand.

An aboriginal guide tells traditional stories at Uluru (Ayers Rock) in Northern Territory.

KEY DATA

Area:	7,686,850km²
Population:	19,520,000
Capital City:	Canberra, Australian Capital Territory
Other Main Cities:	Sydney, Melbourne, Brisbane, Perth
Currency:	Australian Dollar (A$)
GDP Per Capita:	US$26,552*
Highest Point:	Mount Kosciusko (2,228m)

*(2001) Calculated on Purchasing Power Parity basis
Source: World Bank

THE AUSTRALIAN ENVIRONMENT

Giant termite mounds in the Tanami Desert, Northern Territory.

Australia has a widely varied landscape, ranging from rocky uplands to flat lowland plains, and from barren deserts to tropical offshore reefs. On the whole it is an arid country, so green grasslands and lush forests are found only in limited areas.

THE LIE OF THE LAND

Australia's landmass has four distinctive features:

- Despite its huge size, it is a 'low' continent – the highest point is only 2,228m.
- It is an ancient and stable island with few recently-formed rocks. There is no present-day volcanic activity and fault movements are rare.
- There are vast expanses of relatively flat land. This is because erosion has worn down the landscape over many millions of years.
- Landforms change very slowly due to the generally dry climate. Vigorous carving of valleys and gorges is restricted to the moister eastern uplands and temperate Tasmania.

LANDSCAPE FEATURES

INDONESIA

PAPUA NEW GUINEA

Timor

Arafura Sea

Torres Strait

Timor Sea

N

Gulf of Carpentaria

Cape York Peninsula

Great Barrier Reef

Coral Sea

Kimberley Plateau

Barkly Tableland

Carpentaria Lowlands

GREAT SANDY DESERT

TANAMI DESERT

Selwyn Range

Hamersley Range

Macdonnell Ranges

CENTRAL LOWLANDS (GREAT ARTESIAN BASIN)

GREAT DIVIDING RANGE

Tropic of Capricorn

GIBSON DESERT

Uluru ▲ (Ayers Rock) (867m)

SIMPSON DESERT

Fraser Island

WESTERN PLATEAU

GREAT VICTORIA DESERT

Lake Eyre

Darling Downs

Swan

Nullarbor Plain

Lake Torrens

Lake Everard Lake Gairdner

Flinders Range

Darling

Great Australian Bight

Murray

Murrumbidgee

Mt. Kosciusko (2,228m)▲ Snowy Mountains

| 0 | 500 | 1000km |
| 0 | | 600 miles |

Bass Strait

Tasman Sea

Mt. Ossa ▲ (1,617m)

TASMANIA

UPLANDS

Australia's upland areas are low compared to mountain ranges in most other countries. Nevertheless, they form impressive landscapes that vary physically from place to place.

THE GREAT DIVIDING RANGE

Australia's largest continuous upland range runs in an arc for 4,000km from the Cape York Peninsula to southern Victoria, following the east coast of the continent. It is known as the Great Dividing Range, though today it is not as massive as this name suggests because the rocks have been worn down by erosion. Even the most rugged regions, such as the Snowy Mountains in the south, are mostly below 2,000m. The highest peak is Mount Kosciusko, at 2,228m. In Queensland, few areas rise above 1,000m and there are broad plateaux and tablelands, separated by lines of hills.

The Great Dividing Range is asymmetrical. A steep edge faces the coast, while the inland slopes are gentler, sinking steadily to the Central Lowlands. Rivers have cut deeply into the eastern slopes, producing some stunning scenery such as Queensland's Mossman Gorge. Although Australia's east coast has many superb beaches, including Bondi and Fraser Island (the world's largest sand island), the coastal lowlands are generally narrow. In many districts, the hills slope directly to the sea.

INTERIOR RANGES

There are a number of hill ranges scattered across Australia. Examples are the Flinders Range in South Australia, the Macdonnell Ranges in Northern Territory, the Selwyn Range in Queensland and the Hammersley Range in Western Australia. Most are arranged in ridges or clusters, often separated by tablelands or valleys. They appear higher than they actually are because they rise suddenly from vast areas of flat land. Many are built of ancient rocks that contain valuable minerals including silver, copper, nickel, lead and zinc.

TASMANIA

During the last ice age, when sea levels were lower, Tasmania was joined to mainland Australia. Today it is separated by the water of the Bass Strait. Apart from a low coastal plain in the north, Tasmania is a mountainous island. Along the western side there are steep hills called the Tasmanian Ridges. Much of the centre and east of the island is made up of plateaux of resistant rocks, such as the Lakes Plateau. Between these blocks is a zone of lower land called the Midlands Plain, worn down from less resistant rocks.

Tasmania is the only part of Australia that was cold enough for vast icefields and glaciers to grow during the last ice age. The ice vigorously eroded the land, creating rugged terrain and numerous lakes. Lake St Clair, the deepest lake in Australia, lies in a cavernous glacial trough. Today, rain falls year-round on the western mountain ridges and fast-running streams continue to wear away the rocks.

The Macdonnell Ranges rise in rocky ridges near Glen Helen Gorge, west of Alice Springs.

LOWLANDS

Australia's huge north–south lowland zone can
be divided into three main regions, each based
on wide-ranging river drainage systems.

THE CARPENTARIA LOWLANDS

Fringing the Gulf of Carpentaria on the north coast
of the continent, the remote Carpentaria lowlands
are made up of gently sloping, poorly-drained plains
and tropical wetlands. The flat terrain is interrupted
occasionally by low sandstone plateaux.

THE GREAT ARTESIAN BASIN

The Great Artesian Basin – so named because of
the water-bearing rocks that underlie it (see page 33)
– measures approximately 1,600km from north to
south and 1,200km from east to west. The area
is covered by a network of non-permanent streams
that run south-west into Lake Eyre.

The climate becomes increasingly dry towards the
west and the landscape reflects this change. In the
east and centre of the basin the main landforms are
wide, flat floodplains of sand, gravel and pebbles.
These are separated by low, flat-topped hills, mostly
sandstone. Across the western section of the region
there are huge desert landscapes. These include
sandy surfaces such as the Simpson Desert, north of
Lake Eyre, and flat, stony surfaces such as the Sturt
Stony Desert to the east. Lake Eyre itself is empty for
much of the time and you are most likely to see it
as broad sheets of silt and salt flats, known as playas.

THE MURRAY-DARLING BASIN

The drainage area of the River Murray and its
major tributaries – the River Darling and the River
Murrumbidgee – forms a broad lowland plain. The
rivers collect most of their water in the rainy uplands
of the Great Dividing Range and they have year-round
flows that vary from season to season. During heavy
rains there is regular flooding and expansive marshy
surfaces have formed. Sediment arriving at the
mouth of the River Murray near Adelaide has helped
to create sand dunes and offshore sand bars along
the south-east coast of South Australia.

The sandy plains of the Simpson Desert remain largely
arid, except for brief spells after irregular winter rains.

PLAINS AND PLATEAUX

For some 3.5 million km^2 across the arid western half of Australia, wide open landscape is typical. If you drive across in a four-wheel-drive vehicle (essential due to lack of surfaced roads) you will experience long, monotonous hours when nothing seems to change. But occasionally you'll see sudden contrasts that interrupt the flatness, such as a set of steep, red-rock hills or a white, dried-up lakebed shimmering in the heat. Subtle variations crop up too, though you may not notice them at first.

If you take a much broader view, say from an aircraft, it is possible to group this environment into three landscape types: sandy surfaces, stony surfaces, and broad areas of bare, solid rock. The most common of these, covering 1 million km^2, is sand – either sand plains or sand dunes. The dunes can be arc-shaped, but they mostly run in straight lines. In these massive linear dunefields, individual dunes may stretch for 20km and the crests of two parallel dunes may be 1km apart. Over most of Australia's interior, the sand surfaces are held in place by patchy vegetation or hard surface crusts, so moving dunes are rare.

Uluru (Ayers Rock) rises abruptly from a vast area of flat land in the dry 'Red Heart' of the continent.

AN EXTREME CLIMATE

One of the outstanding features of Australia is its dryness. Moister climates are limited to the fringes and the eastern uplands, and rainfall totals decrease rapidly inland. At least one-third of the country has on average less than 250mm annual rainfall, though patterns are unpredictable and totals can vary greatly from year to year. Much of Australia is also consistently hot due to long hours of strong sunshine. This means that an unusually high proportion of rainwater is lost through evaporation.

CLIMATE ZONES

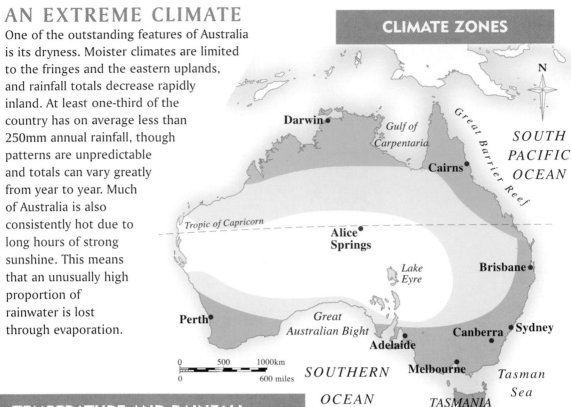

	Tropical and sub-tropical
	Warm temperate
	Semi-arid
	Arid
	Cool temperate

TEMPERATURE AND RAINFALL

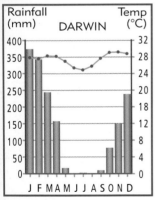

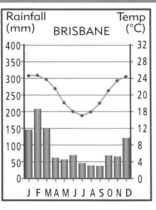

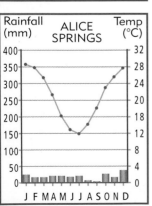

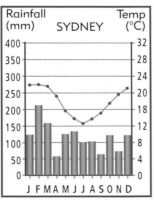

CLIMATIC REGIONS

The map above divides Australia into five generalised climatic regions, based on patterns of rainfall and average temperatures. Each region covers a huge area, so there will be local variation within each one.

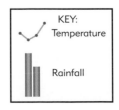

KEY:
Temperature

Rainfall

14

TROPICAL AND SUB-TROPICAL NORTH AND NORTH-EAST

In north and north-eastern Australia, the climate is ruled by the seasonal movement of the tropical monsoon. During the Australian summer (November–March) warm, moist monsoon air sweeps across the north and north-east coasts. Rains come in regular, heavy deluges and can deposit more than 1,600mm a year over the mountains. During the winter the monsoon belt moves northwards and is replaced by hot, dry air that drifts across from inland areas where far less rain falls.

Summer temperatures in the far northern tropics average well over 20°C, and the weather feels hot and 'sticky' due to very high humidities. Winters remain hot with little cloud, and only along the coasts do sea breezes bring relief. People wait anxiously for the first rains to break the heat, which regularly sizzles over 30°C. Yet when the rains do arrive, the humid air makes life exhausting. Moving southwards down the east Queensland coast, the climate becomes sub-tropical and levels of heat and moisture, though high, become less extreme.

CASE STUDY
TROPICAL CYCLONES IN BABINDA, QUEENSLAND

Babinda is a small town on the coast of tropical Queensland. During the summer monsoon season, more than 250mm of rain may fall in one day. In most years at least one tropical cyclone hits the coast and the intensity of wind and rain can be amazing. On one occasion, more than 350mm of rain was recorded to have fallen in a space of seven hours. At the height of this deluge, more than 10mm of rain blasted the town within a five-minute period. During a cyclone, sheets of muddy water pour from nearby agricultural slopes and flood the town. Local people are left to clear the sticky red mud from the streets and fill in deep gullies eroded on the farmland.

Heavy seasonal rain blasts the vegetation of a tropical rainforest in north-east Queensland.

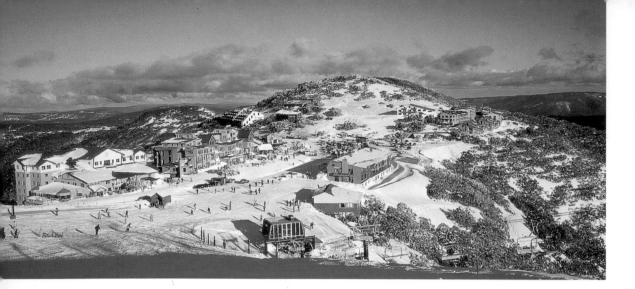

TEMPERATE SOUTH-EAST AND SOUTH-WEST AUSTRALIA

Down the coast from Brisbane, temperatures become more moderate and the seasonal pattern of rainfall changes. In an arc that includes Melbourne, Adelaide and part of the River Murray Basin, most rain comes in winter. For example, in a normal year, 60 per cent of Adelaide's rain falls between May and August.

This seasonal bias is caused by the west–east movement of mid-latitude depressions. These are areas of low pressure that, in winter, bring cloud, rain and some snow to south-west and south-east Australia. In summer they normally pass further south and so bring less rain to the mainland.

The name Snowy Mountains tells us that high areas have regular snow – in some cases enough to support ski resorts. But in non-mountainous areas, temperatures in this zone remain mild in the winter (10–15°C) and rise rapidly during the summer. The summer average is 20–28°C, though there are frequent hotter spells. During the Australian Open Tennis Championship in Melbourne in January 2003, daytime temperatures reached a scorching 34°C. When these heatwaves occur during drought years, there is a high risk of serious bush fires.

The south-west corner of Australia, centred on Perth, enjoys a form of Mediterranean climate, with well-defined mild, damp winters and hot, dry summers. Rainfall totals drop and average temperatures rise rapidly as you move further inland.

ABOVE: Mount Hotham Alpine Resort attracts skiers to the mountains of north-east Victoria.
RIGHT: Hot sun dries and cracks the mud on the northern shore of Lake Eyre in South Australia.

THE ARID/SEMI-ARID INTERIOR

The average rainfall across Australia's huge interior is less than 250mm a year. However, average figures are not always useful because what stands out here is the unreliability of the rainfall. Cattle ranchers in the hot, dry plains know that 400mm of rain one year may be followed by 100mm, or less, the next.

Australia has no extreme deserts and even the driest areas receive some rain. It comes as occasional heavy downpours when monsoon storms stray south from the tropics, or when depressions shift unusually far north. As these moist air masses move inland the air is heated by the hot land surface. Strong convection currents can then cause severe thunderstorms.

In the arid/semi-arid region there are few clouds and days are extended with long hours of sunshine. For at least six months of the year, daytime temperatures may exceed 30°C. At night, the skies are cool and a diurnal range (difference in temperature between day and night) of 20°C is not unusual.

This can be an extremely harsh climate – a difficult one in which to live. Months of dry heat may be broken by heavy rainstorms and sudden flash floods. Then, when the skies clear, any water that does not seep into the ground quickly evaporates and within days the hot, cloudless weather returns.

Bush fires are a real threat in the dry summer heat of much of central and southern Australia.

TEMPERATE TASMANIA

Tasmania lies far enough south to be in the path of the mid-latitude depressions all year round. These depressions have crossed the vast southern oceans and can bring strong winds and continuously cloudy weather. Rain falls in every season, usually with a winter maximum. Except for the south-east corner, Tasmania receives an average rainfall of at least 1,000mm per year. Compared with the rest of Australia, the rain is generally reliable and rivers therefore run year-round. Australians are very fond of 'Tasie' because its moderate, mixed climate and cool running streams are so different from the severe extremes of so much of their country.

Tasmania's temperate environment encourages outdoor leisure activities such us fly-fishing.

A UNIQUE ECOLOGY

Australia has a very distinctive collection of plants and animals, many unique to the continent. For example, there are marsupials such as kangaroos, wallabies, wombats and bandicoots, which carry their young in pouches. One of the joys of walking or camping – especially in the wetter regions – is hearing the songs of a wonderful variety of birds, such as the piercing laugh of the kookaburra. There are giant tree ferns and a wide range of eucalyptus or 'gum' trees, from massive red gums to tall, thin stringybarks with their long strips of hanging grey bark.

VEGETATION REGIONS

Australia can be broadly split into differing vegetation regions, as seen on the map below. In most places the change from one region to another is gradual. Vegetation type is closely related to water availability, temperature and how the plants adapt to the conditions – lush rainforests bloom in tropical monsoon areas, for example, while cacti and bunch grasses survive desert droughts. Many types of eucalyptus and acacia trees grow in surprisingly dry areas, though the less water there is, the smaller and sparser they become.

A baby kangaroo, or 'joey', will not leave its mother's pouch until it is able to fend for itself.

VEGETATION AND SURFACE TYPES

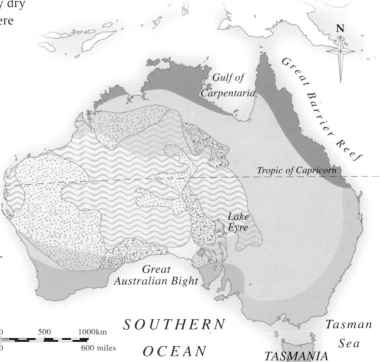

≈ Sand plains and dunes

Stony plains

Broad rock surfaces

Tropical monsoon woodland and rainforest

Temperate woodland and forest

Dry savannah with short grasses, scrub and scattered trees

Drought-resistant open woodland and scrub

Sparse desert vegetation

N

Gulf of Carpentaria

Great Barrier Reef

Tropic of Capricorn

Lake Eyre

Great Australian Bight

SOUTHERN OCEAN

Tasman Sea

TASMANIA

0   500   1000km
0   600 miles

LEFT: Eucalyptus trees, such as these in the Karri Forest, Western Australia, can grow to over 60m.

RIGHT: The kookaburra – a type of king-fisher – is unique to the Australian continent.

EXAMPLES OF AUSTRALIA'S ECOLOGICAL DIVERSITY

Eucalypts ('gum trees')	More than 500 species
Acacias ('wattles')	More than 600 species
Marsupials	More than 120 species
Snakes	160 species, of which two-thirds are venomous
Parrots	50 species
Cockatoos	11 species, out of only 12 in the world
Dingos	Claimed to be the world's oldest wild dog species
Fish	More than 2,000 species, including 90 species of sharks

EFFECTS OF ISOLATION

Australia's unusual species have evolved because the island has been isolated from other landmasses for many millions of years. This has allowed the plants and animals to adapt well to local conditions. For example, kangaroos and wallabies have developed strong rear legs and bounding movements to help them travel long distances in search of food and water. They can also stretch upwards to reach leaves from shrubs and trees. Koala, in aboriginal language, means 'I don't drink', because eucalyptus leaves – the only things koalas eat – provide all the moisture they need.

Another important legacy of Australia's isolation is that native animals and birds have evolved as part of a distinct ecosystem. They have developed survival techniques based on local predator-prey relationships – but they are highly vulnerable when new species are introduced from abroad. Many such species have been introduced since European settlers arrived in 1788. Because they come from different ecosystems and have no natural predators in Australia, most have thrived. Animals such as cattle, sheep, foxes, dogs, cats, rats and mice compete with native species for food. The best-known intruder is the rabbit. Today its population is counted in the hundreds of millions and it has become a national plague (see page 52).

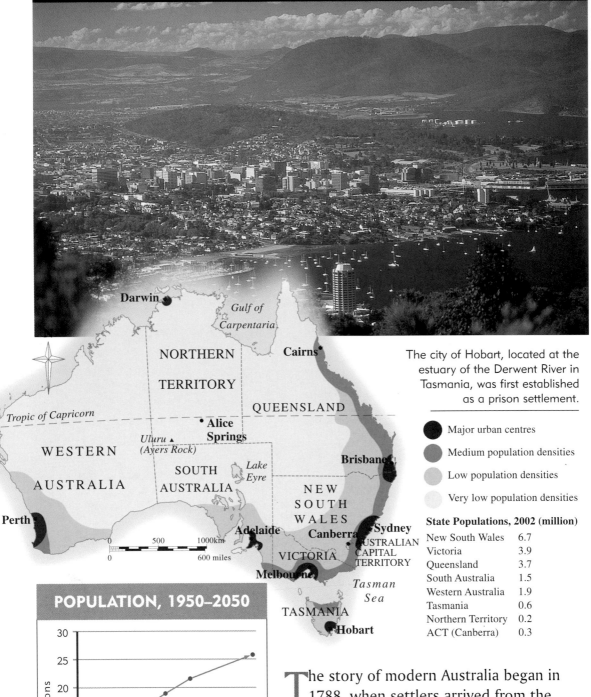

The city of Hobart, located at the estuary of the Derwent River in Tasmania, was first established as a prison settlement.

- Major urban centres
- Medium population densities
- Low population densities
- Very low population densities

State Populations, 2002 (million)

New South Wales	6.7
Victoria	3.9
Queensland	3.7
South Australia	1.5
Western Australia	1.9
Tasmania	0.6
Northern Territory	0.2
ACT (Canberra)	0.3

POPULATION, 1950–2050

Millions

Sources: UN Population Division, *Geographical Digest*, UNDP

* =estimates

The story of modern Australia began in 1788, when settlers arrived from the British Isles. As recently as 1950 there were fewer than 9 million people living on the continent. By mid-2003 the total had reached 19.9 million, and by 2050 there may be 25 million Australians. In comparison, the UK is only one-thirtieth of the size of Australia, but has a population of more than 59 million.

POPULATION CLUSTERS

The Australian population is very unevenly distributed. Eight out of ten people live on only 2 per cent of the land and within 80km of the coast. At the other extreme, barely 500,000 people are scattered across 80 per cent of the continent. Two out of three Australians live in or near the six state capitals.

SETTLEMENT PATTERNS

Before the federation of states was established, Australia was divided into separate British colonies, each with its own capital. Several, such as Hobart and Brisbane, began as prison settlements. Until well into the nineteenth century, convicts from the UK were transported to prisons in Australia. Many stayed on as settlers when they were released.

Immigrants in colonial times arrived by ship, so ports such as Sydney and Perth became the main towns. As the economy grew, farming and mineral products were exported through these ports. New settlements and transport routes spread slowly inland, but populations clustered mainly around the coasts. During the 1990s, two-thirds of Australia's population growth was focussed on four major centres – Sydney, Melbourne, Perth and Brisbane. The most rapid growth occurs at the edges of urban areas and in attractive coastal and mountain regions.

POPULATION GROWTH

At present, Australia's population is growing by about 1.3 per cent a year. This growth is explained by two components: natural change (the difference between numbers of births and deaths, usually expressed as a rate per 1,000 population) and migration (the movement of people in and out of the country). The table (above right) shows how this worked in 2002, when Australia's population grew by 252,000.

NATURAL CHANGE

As in most countries, Australia's birth rates are falling. In 1995, there were 14.2 births per 1,000 population. By 2001 this had dropped to 13. Meanwhile, mortality (death) rates have stayed at around 6.9 per 1,000 people. So the number of births still exceeds the number of deaths, creating a natural increase.

But to sustain a population over time, fertility rates need to be at least two live births per woman. Australia's average is less than this. So, although deaths among infants are decreasing (see graph below), there are still too few people in the younger age groups. This means that immigration will become increasingly important if Australia's population is to continue to grow.

POPULATION CHANGE DURING 2002

NATURAL CHANGE

Births	247,000
Deaths	133,000
Natural increase	114,000

MIGRATION

Immigrants	358,000
Emigrants	220,000
Net migration	138,000

TOTAL CHANGE
114,000 + 138,000 = 252,000

Source: Australian Government Website

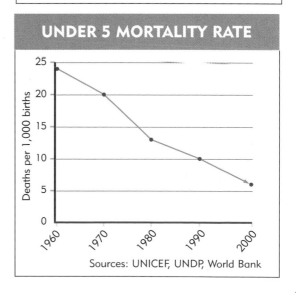

UNDER 5 MORTALITY RATE

Deaths per 1,000 births

Sources: UNICEF, UNDP, World Bank

Melbourne's thriving Chinatown is evidence of the city's substantial immigrant population.

ORIGIN OF IMMIGRANT RESIDENTS IN AUSTRALIA, 2001

COUNTRY	NUMBER
UK	1,210,000
New Zealand	375,000
Italy	242,000
Former Yugoslavia	210,100
Vietnam	175,000
China	168,000
Greece	141,000
Philippines	123,000

Source: Australian Government Website

MIGRATION

Migration is the movement of people to and from a given place. The difference between numbers of immigrants (those who come in) and emigrants (those who leave) is known as the net migration balance. In Australia, there have generally been more immigrants than emigrants, and this has been important to population growth.

In the mid-twentieth century, immigration was based on a 'White Australia' policy. The government was worried that Australia's

CASE STUDY
THE PIAZZA FAMILY FROM ITALY

Ron Piazza lives in a Brisbane suburb and has a job at a civil engineering company. His father migrated from Italy during the 1950s and worked on sugar farms and banana plantations in northern Queensland. Italians were popular employees because they were willing to work in the hot climate. Ron's father lived in a small town near Cairns, where he met and married a girl from Italy. He worked on sugar farms for 20 years, and they had three children – Ron,

Maria and Joe. By 1980 sugar production was becoming more mechanised and Ron's parents were getting older. So the family moved to an Italian neighbourhood in Brisbane. The parents ran a bakery and pasta shop until they retired. They now live in a small retirement community on the Queensland coast.

Ron and his brother and sister have all visited Italy but they speak little Italian. They all graduated from Australian universities. Maria and her Lebanese husband run a travel agency in Darwin, and Joe is a supermarket manager in Melbourne.

relatively small population would be overwhelmed by migrants from Asia's rapidly growing populations. By 1970 this policy was abandoned and Australia today is a multicultural society. In 2001, 4.5 million people in Australia were foreign-born.

Foreign immigrants in Australia may take language classes to assist their integration.

THE REFUGEE PROBLEM

Australia is an attractive country both for voluntary migrants and for refugees fleeing their countries. This has caused strong arguments about the growing numbers of asylum seekers. There have been several waves of illegal immigrants into Australia. In 2001 the Australian Navy stopped boatloads of Afghan refugees from landing in Northern Territory.

POPULATION STRUCTURE

Australia has a 'mature' population structure – most people are in the family-raising age range of 20–50 years. High quality healthcare means low infant mortality rates – but fewer babies are now being born, life expectancies are rising and so the population is ageing. It is likely that by 2015 at least 15 per cent of the population will be over 65. The figure will be higher if immigration decreases because migrants are often young people with large families.

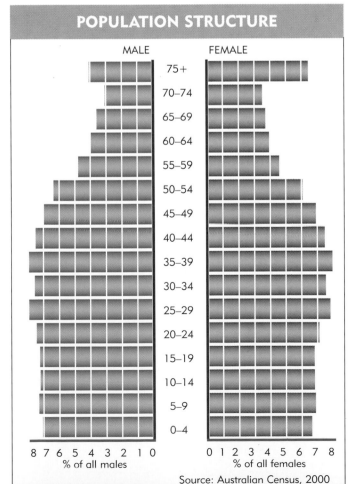

POPULATION STRUCTURE

MALE — FEMALE

75+
70–74
65–69
60–64
55–59
50–54
45–49
40–44
35–39
30–34
25–29
20–24
15–19
10–14
5–9
0–4

8 7 6 5 4 3 2 1 0
% of all males

0 1 2 3 4 5 6 7 8
% of all females

Source: Australian Census, 2000

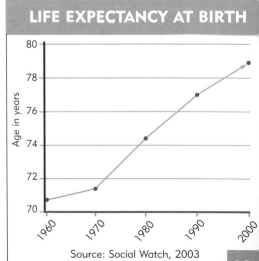

LIFE EXPECTANCY AT BIRTH

Age in years

80
78
76
74
72
70

1960 1970 1980 1990 2000

Source: Social Watch, 2003

THE ABORIGINAL POPULATION

There were probably 300,000 Aborigines spread throughout Australia in 1788. But the 1981 Census recorded barely 200,000 people as Aborigines. In the 2001 Census, however, numbers had risen again to 458,500. This is because people of mixed descent as well as full-blood Aborigines are now counted as 'aboriginal'. The aboriginal story falls into three broad chapters, as follows.

PRE-EUROPEAN: UP TO 1788

Aborigines have lived in Australia for at least 50,000 years. They were originally semi-nomadic people who circulated in small tribal groups, or 'bands'. They moved over terratorial 'homelands' to find food and water, and developed a close relationship with the environment. According to tradition, the homeland belonged to the tribal group (not to individuals) forever, and it had deep religious meaning.

EXCLUSION AND OPPRESSION: 1788–1950

European settlement brought disaster to the Aborigines:

- They were pushed off their lands and denied legal rights. Many bands were crowded on to government reservations or Christian missions. Some stayed as stockmen or farmworkers.
- Government and missionary policies discouraged or banned traditional ways of life and even languages.
- Aboriginal peoples had no resistance to diseases such as smallpox and measles, introduced by Europeans.
- Europeans misunderstood Australian conditions. They overused the land, killed wildlife and sapped water supplies. They degraded the environmental resources on which Aborigines depended.

An aboriginal guide leads tourists on the 'Liru Walk' through groves of flowering mulla mulla plants near Uluru (Ayers Rock).

FORCES FOR REVIVAL

Aboriginals and 'aboriginal pride' movements today campaign for:

- Full citizenship and the right to vote.
- Improved housing, health and education conditions, leading to better job opportunities.
- Legal rights to traditional homelands.
- Reduction of prejudice and increased respect for aboriginal cultures.

THE STRUGGLE FOR REVIVAL: SINCE 1950

Aboriginal organisations have recently been working hard to revive their traditional culture, fighting especially for legal land rights and aboriginal pride. Strong efforts are also being made by the Australian government and citizens to correct the wrongs done to the aboriginal people.

The aboriginal population is growing once more, but Aborigines are still the poorest group in Australian society. Increasing numbers are moving to urban areas – most of New South Wales's 135,000 Aborigines live in and around Sydney. Only one in three Aborigines now remain in rural districts – the majority of these are found in remote parts

The Aboriginal Art and Culture Centre in Alice Springs promotes traditional tribal customs. It is owned and run by a local aboriginal group.

of Northern Territory and Western Australia, where some traditional ways of life may be maintained. As legal land rights are extended, aboriginal pride grows and more jobs become available, more aboriginal people are moving back to their original homelands.

CASE STUDY
THE NORTHERN LAND COUNCIL

Unfortunately tensions remain between aboriginal and European interests. Across vast areas of Australia's dry interior, ranchers rent grazing land from the government. They have campaigned to 'extinguish' all remaining aboriginal land rights. Aboriginal bodies fight for the reverse position – for permanent

rights to the homelands – and they have won several important legal battles in recent years. The Northern Land Council (NLC) is one such organisation. It was set up in 1973 to support traditional aboriginal landowners and other aboriginal people in Arnhem Land, Northern Territory. The NLC has regained legal title to its homelands and now leases one section to a uranium mining corporation and another large expanse to the government as the Kakadu National Park. These bring in money and jobs.

URBAN AUSTRALIA

A commercial street in Adelaide that has benefited from refurbishment.

Nine out of ten Australians today live in urban areas. These include great cities, suburban settlements, resorts, retirement communities and market and service towns scattered across the continent. The state capitals accommodate at least 50 per cent of the population. With the exception of Canberra, Australian Capital Territory, the capitals are all sited on natural harbours and act as major ports.

URBAN POPULATION

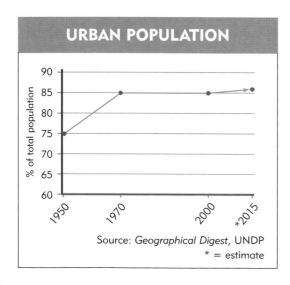

Source: *Geographical Digest*, UNDP
* = estimate

AUSTRALIAN CAPITAL TERRITORY

When Australia was united into a single nation in 1901, the city of Canberra was planned. It was built in the mountains of New South Wales and was given its own 'territory', or state. Canberra is the only major Australian city not on the coast. Today it is the seat of the Commonwealth government, with the formal title of Canberra, Australian Capital Territory (ACT). Despite its beautiful mountain setting, its inland position has not been able to compete with Sydney or Melbourne in attracting businesses or industries.

RECENT TRENDS

During the 1990s, 70 per cent of Australia's total population growth (equal to 830,000 people) occurred in and around Sydney, Melbourne, Perth and Brisbane. Australia's population is becoming increasingly concentrated in this way. For example, the Queensland coastal strip from Brisbane south to the New South Wales border is known as the Gold Coast. In 1970 it was a string of small beachside resorts. Today it is a 100km built-up strip of commuter, retirement and resort cities such as Surfers Paradise. Between 1991 and 2001, the total Gold Coast population exploded from 226,000 to a staggering 400,000.

The most rapid growth is in the outer towns. For example, the spread of Melbourne south-west around Port Phillip Bay has reached Geelong (see page 30). People and businesses move out from the older central cities. They are replaced by migrants from other regions of Australia and from abroad. Young people and recent immigrants are most likely to live in central cities. Families and older people move outwards to the suburbs and smaller towns.

In recent years the cities' Central Business Districts (CBDs) have grown, creating more jobs. Office space in downtown Perth doubled during the 1990s. Older, inner districts have been improved, or 'gentrified', attracting wealthier people and fashionable businesses including cafés and boutiques.

ABOVE: Surfers Paradise is just one of the ever-expanding resorts on the east Queensland coast.

RIGHT: Towering modern office blocks dominate the Perth skyline.

SMALL-TOWN AUSTRALIA

Meanwhile, many rural towns in Australia are suffering serious decline. Agriculture is changing and recently has been less prosperous, farmers and other rural people are increasingly mobile, and in many districts there are few jobs or career opportunities. Many smaller market towns are losing their function. Between 1990 and 2000, 50 per cent of towns with fewer than 5,000 people declined (see page 40).

Two types of town are avoiding these problems. Firstly, there are those within commuting distance of big cities or with accessible locations along main transport routes – towns up to 50km around Adelaide and along the Sydney–Melbourne road corridor, for example. This is part of a counterurbanisation process where people and businesses move from cities to smaller urban settlements for lower costs, improved standards of living and better working environments. Secondly, there are towns that are attractive to tourists and for retirement. Examples of these are found along the coastal zone between Brisbane and Rockhampton (Queensland) and north of Perth (Western Australia).

Sydney Harbour, with the Opera House left of the CBD, and the Harbour Bridge to the right.

Sydney is the capital of New South Wales and Australia's largest city. It is situated around a magnificent harbour, which is actually the estuary of the River Parramatta. The original settlement along the south side of the estuary is the site of the modern CBD, which boasts two of the world's best-known structures – the Sydney Harbour Bridge and the Opera House.

Modern Sydney covers the harbour basin, runs inland along the Parramatta valley and spills across the surrounding hills. As in all Australian cities, away from the centre the suburbs consist mainly of well-spaced one- and two-storey homes. Most affluent districts are in the hills north of the harbour. During the 1990s, Sydney's population grew at an average of 1.3 per cent a year. By 2021 there are likely to be 5 million inhabitants, with a demand for 500,000 extra homes. There is concern over the environmental impact of continued expansion. Lifestyles are water-oriented, based around the wonderful beaches and bays – the resort of Manly at the north entrance of the harbour, for example, is a popular commuter town.

Sydney lies at the centre of an urbanised region that runs 180km along the New South Wales coast from the coal and industrial port of Newcastle (population 300,000) to industrial Greater Wollongong (population 250,000). This is the most prosperous region of Australia. Sydney itself has 20 per cent of the country's population but 25 per cent of the income. Sydney is the main gateway for people, trade and finance. The prosperity is based on the so-called 'new economy', moving away from manufacturing to business, finance and information services. During the 1990s, 50,000 new jobs were created in the city, mostly in high-skilled business, science and technology

NEW

Wollemi N.P.

N

SOUTH

Orange

GREAT DIVIDING RANGE

Blue Mountains

Newcastle

Brisbane Waters N.P.

Gosford

WALES

Sydney Harbour

Blue Mts. N.P.

Sydney CBD

Sydney

Lake Burragorang

Royal N.P.

Tasman

To Melbourne

Wollongong

Sea

Port Kembla

Main urban area

- - - Commuter fringe

National parks

Resorts, holiday homes, commuter towns

0   100   200km

0   100 miles

SYDNEY STATISTICS

- Headquarters of 60 of Australia's top 100 companies.
- 60 per cent of CBD workers are in business, financial and property services.
- Jobs in law and accounting professions increased by 60 per cent in the 1990s.
- One in two government jobs for the metropolitan region are in the city's CBD.
- 55 per cent of all international visitors to Australia pass through Sydney Airport.
- In 2001, more than 2.5 million visitors stayed in the city.

A monorail and pedestrian bridge make Sydney's CBD highly accessible to commuters.

professions. Sydney has overtaken Melbourne as Australia's business and finance capital. In 2001, 250 global corporations had their Australian headquarters in Sydney, compared with just 83 in Melbourne. Sydney has truly become a 'global city', especially since it staged the 2000 Olympic Games.

Cockle Bay Wharf on Darling Harbour is just one of Sydney's popular recreation areas.

Each year Sydney attracts 40 per cent of all immigrants to Australia. In the district of Erskineville, one in two schoolchildren are from ethnic minority groups and there is a successful Chinatown on the edge of the CBD. Many immigrants from Hong Kong, Singapore and Malaysia are professionals who have settled in the wealthier suburbs of north Sydney. Poorer, less skilled immigrants, often from Vietnam, Indonesia and China, live in older, inner suburbs in south Sydney.

As in all modern cities, increasing numbers of families have moved out to the suburbs and 50 per cent of Sydney's workforce now commutes. The inner districts are refilled with newcomers, such as immigrants and young Australians. Regeneration projects have led to the gentrification of some older areas as increasing numbers of professionals move in. These include disued industrial buildings along the River Parramatta, and The Rocks, a fashionable district by the bayfront.

Located beside the Yarra River, Melbourne is a dynamic city that competes with Sydney in terms of business, leisure and transport facilities.

Melbourne is the capital of Victoria, Australia's second – largest city and one of the country's earliest settlements. The original town was built by the mouth of the Yarra River, at the head of Port Phillip Bay where the CBD stands today – and the commercial port grew up nearby at Port Melbourne. The huge bay is a fine harbour and gives shelter from the storms that sweep through the Bass Strait.

Modern Melbourne and its sprawling suburbs extend around the bay and across the coastal floodplain, especially to the east. There are superb beaches, landscaped parks, golf courses where kangaroos graze, and top-class stadiums, including the Melbourne Cricket Ground. The spacious suburbs are comfortably shaded by trees. One of the city's attractive features is its public transport system. There is an efficient, cheap network of rail, light rail, tram and bus routes.

Melbourne people, like most Australians, enjoy relaxing outdoors, and a string of beachfront towns and marinas stretches south-east as far as Phillip Island. This island, about the size of the Isle of Wight, is an easy day-trip for locals, and a popular holiday destination. Attractions include beaches where fairy penguins can be seen each day, and the island has the circuit for the Australian car and motorcycle grand prix races.

Between 1991 and 2001, Melbourne's population increased from 2.7 million to 3.2 million – 70 per cent of Victoria's total. The rest of Victoria grew much more slowly. One-third of Melbourne's growth came from immigration, and in 2001 more than one in five residents were born outside Australia. There are

Map labels:

VICTORIA

Ballarat

Melbourne
Melbourne CBD

Brisbane Ranges N.P.

Geelong

Port Phillip Bay

Otway N.P.

Ferry links with Tasmania

Phillip Island

Wilson's Promontory N.P.

To Sydney

Main urban area
Commuter fringe
National parks
Resorts, holiday homes, commuter towns

N

0   50   100km
0   50 miles

B a s s   S t r a i t

Crowds gather by the water at Victoria Harbour in Melbourne's redeveloped docklands.

communities of Greeks, Italians and Lebanese who arrived in large numbers, especially during the 1970s and 1980s. More people of Greek origin live in Melbourne than in any other city outside Greece itself. More recently the main flows have been from South-east Asia and the Pacific islands. Many young people from Tasmania are also attracted to the city because of the direct ferry routes.

Melbourne generates 18 per cent of Australia's GDP. More than 80 multinational corporations have their Australian head offices in the fast-growing CBD. Greater Melbourne is more industrial than Sydney, despite a recent decline in manufacturing industries such as textiles and motor vehicles. Engineering businesses, petro-chemical complexes and the modern port facilities are mainly located to the west of the city, as far as Geelong.

As in Sydney, Melbourne's older inner districts are being regenerated. Derelict docks have been redeveloped for residential and leisure uses – for example, there is a very large casino along the riverfront close to the CBD, developed in part to attract tourists away from Sydney. Parts of old Port Melbourne have been gentrified – disused warehouses and other commercial buildings have become fashionable apartments, workshops and studios, and parks and cycle-ways weave through the district. Part of the attraction is the long beach and the light rail route that takes commuters and shoppers to the CBD in just 15 minutes. The main ferry terminal for Tasmania is Port Melbourne's only link with its maritime past.

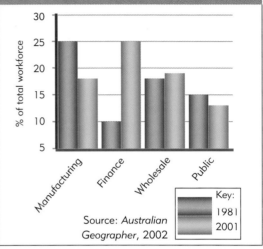

MELBOURNE'S MAIN ECONOMIC SECTORS

y-axis: % of total workforce (5–30)

x-axis: Manufacturing, Finance, Wholesale, Public

Source: *Australian Geographer*, 2002

Key:
1981
2001

Sydney and Melbourne are rivals. However, a survey in 2001 concluded that they are equal but different. Melbourne is well-placed to be the leading port and its capacity to move goods is far superior to that of Sydney. It is well located too, for what manufacturing remains in Australia. Sydney is primarily a financial and producer services centre. Easy transportation and communication between the two cities means that they can both benefit from each other's strengths.

Melbourne's light rail system is one of Australia's most efficient transport services.

AGRICULTURAL AND RURAL AUSTRALIA

Cattle grazing on the rolling pastures around Merrijig, north-east Victoria.

Outside the big cities, Australia becomes a vast rural country, sparsely scattered with small communities and isolated farmsteads. Farmlands range from intensive crop plantations to remote, dry expanses where only hardy cattle find grazing. There is a sense of space and emptiness about much of rural Australia.

WATER – THE VITAL RESOURCE

As we've seen, Australia is a dry continent – three-quarters of the country receives on average less than 500mm of rain a year and in many regions the rainfall is highly seasonal and unreliable. As a result, water availability is the crucial control on agriculture.

RIVER NETWORKS

The country's lack of rainfall is reflected in its river systems. Permanent streams that give year-round surface water are limited to the moister fringes and Tasmania. Elsewhere, streams are either seasonal – flowing during the wetter months – or ephemeral – flowing briefly after occasional storms.

DAMS AND RESERVOIRS

In relatively rainy areas, water can be stored behind dams in reservoirs. These supply water to farms and settlements downstream. Larger schemes, such as the Tinaroo Falls Dam in Queensland, often include hydroelectric power generation (HEP). One problem is loss of water through evaporation – the huge Lake Eildon reservoir in the headwaters of the River Murray (Victoria) is generally less than half full, partly because the Sun's powerful heat evaporates the water.

RIVER TO RIVER

Basin transfer is the transfer of water from one river basin with a surplus to another where demand exceeds supply. This involves costly engineering schemes but it is a useful way of distributing water. The largest and most famous system is the Snowy Mountains Project in New South Wales, built in the 1960s. Tunnels cut through the Great Dividing Range transfer water from rivers running coastwards, to headwater streams of the Murray Basin. HEP generators supply power to Canberra and the Sydney region.

ABOVE: Lake Kununurra and its dam store and divert water from the Ord River in Kimberley, Western Australia.

RIGHT: HEP generation at the Murray Power Station, part of the Snowy Mountains Project, New South Wales.

UNDERGROUND RESERVES

An alternative source of water is found, in some regions, beneath the surface. This groundwater is stored in aquifers – layers of rock that can retain water. The water arrives as rain in mountain areas, sinks into the ground and moves slowly through the aquifers. The largest of these groundwater stores is the Great Artesian Basin of New South Wales and Queensland. Wells have been drilled into the aquifers to allow agriculture to extend further into arid inland areas.

WATER AVAILABILITY REGIONS

We can divide Australia into four broad regions according to the main features of their water availability:

- Regions with sufficient surface and near-surface water to support plant growth through much of the year – for example Tasmania and the Great Dividing Range.

- Less moist regions with permanent stream networks to sustain water tables and supply irrigation systems – for example the River Murray Basin.
- Semi-arid regions with artesian groundwater that can be pumped out for irrigation and animals – for example the Great Artesian Basin in Queensland.
- Arid regions with ephemeral streams and few groundwater resources – for example much of the interior, sometimes known as the 'Red Heart', of the continent.

CHANGING IMPORTANCE

In 1900, agriculture produced 23 per cent of Australia's GDP, but by 2000 this had plummeted to 3 per cent. In 1970, 45 per cent of the country's export value came from agricultural products, but this had more than halved by 2001. Today, fewer than 400,000 Australians are employed in agriculture, yet it is still a major industry. Four products lead the export rankings – meat, wool, grains, and grapes for wine. Cattle numbers are on the increase, cereal output is rising and arable land continues to expand.

AGRICULTURAL REGIONS

Australia's agricultural regions are dominated by two features. Firstly, cropland generally decreases and grazing increases as you move further inland. Secondly, the drier the environment, the less intensive the farming.

AUSTRALIA'S LEADING AGRICULTURAL EXPORTS, 2001

	OUTPUT (tonnes)	VALUE (A$ billion)	WORLD RANKING
Meat and animals	1.5 million	5.0	5th
Wheat and flour	15.8 million	3.2	2nd
Wool and wool yarn	465,000	2.2	1st

Source: *International Trade Statistics Yearbook*, 2002

CROPS AND INTENSIVE ANIMAL REARING

Part of the Queensland coast lies within the tropics. A wide range of crops is grown there, but the main commercial products are sugar and tropical fruits such as bananas, paw paws and pineapples. Maize and alfalfa are grown as cattle feed for ranches inland. Southwards, where the climate becomes more temperate, wheat, barley, apples, pears, and grass for hay and silage are increasingly important.

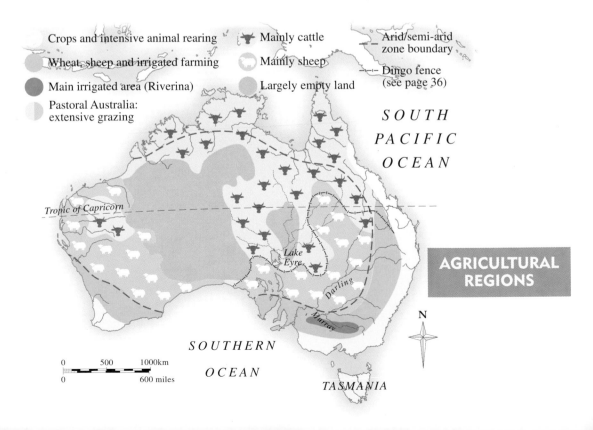

Crops and intensive animal rearing

Wheat, sheep and irrigated farming

Main irrigated area (Riverina)

Pastoral Australia: extensive grazing

Mainly cattle

Mainly sheep

Largely empty land

Arid/semi-arid zone boundary

Dingo fence (see page 36)

SOUTH PACIFIC OCEAN

Tropic of Capricorn

Lake Eyre

Darling

Murray

N

AGRICULTURAL REGIONS

SOUTHERN OCEAN

0   500   1000km
0   600 miles

TASMANIA

Around major cities there is a zone of market gardening and dairy farms that supply the urban markets. But 60 per cent of Australia's dairy industry is concentrated in the moist, temperate districts of Victoria. Since 1970, production has doubled while the number of dairy farmers has fallen from 26,000 to fewer than 8,000.

Tasmania's climate is well suited to crops such as potatoes, apples, wheat and hay, as well as dairy and beef cattle. There are 2,700 hectares of apple orchards, producing over 50,000 tonnes of fruit per year. Most are exported, the main markets being South-east Asia and Scandinavia.

CASE STUDY
FARMING CHANGE IN NORTH QUEENSLAND

Mechanised harvesting of sugar cane near Innisfail in the far north of Queensland.

The Mareeba-Dimbula Irrigation Area (MDIA) comprises some 15,000 hectares of land in north-east Queensland, irrigated by a reservoir called Lake Tinaroo. In 1985 there were 400 farm holdings in the MDIA, and most gave tobacco as their main product. Government quota and marketing policies limited the tobacco area to 4,000 hectares, in an effort to protect local producers and maintain tobacco prices. So farmers diversified, switching to cereals such as rice and maize, vegetables including peanuts and soya beans, various fruits, and intensive beef cattle rearing.

By 2000, the farming system had changed. The irrigated area had grown by 50 per cent but tobacco had collapsed. Farmers now grew sugar cane, orchard fruits such as avocados and mangoes, and vegetables. Sugar cane covered 4,800 hectares compared with less than 300 hectares in 1985. The following three main factors explain these changes:

- **Government policy**: in 1995, after smoking-related health concerns had notably reduced demand, tobacco growing was deregulated. Quotas and price supports ended and the crop now has to compete on a global level.
- **Scale of production**: without government support, local tobacco growers are too small in scale to compete in world markets. In contrast, the Queensland sugar industry is an efficient, large-scale operation.
- **Accessibility**: improved transport and refrigeration facilities are making the MDIA less remote, so it is easier to farm perishable products. Cairns is the hub of the area.

LEADING MDIA CROPS BY VALUE, 2000 (A$ MILLION)

1. Sugar cane	33
2. Mangoes	30
3. Vegetables	21
4. Avocados	20
5. Tobacco	17

Source: *Australian Geographer*, 2001

WHEAT, SHEEP AND IRRIGATED FARMING

This area (defined on the map on page 34) supports 45 per cent of Australia's sheep and three-quarters of its cereal grains. Most farms include both wheat and sheep and some also rear cattle. The wheat belt in the south of Western Australia, with its 400–700mm of rainfall a year, makes the state Australia's leading wheat producer. More intensive cropping and animal rearing are possible along the Murray valley where irrigation systems are in operation. Except in irrigated districts, most farms are larger than 500 hectares.

RIGHT: Irrigated farmland near Cobram, on the Victoria side of the Murray valley.

PASTORAL AUSTRALIA

Extensive animal grazing dominates more than half of Australia's agricultural land. Here, stocking densities (see page 38) are very low and ranches are huge. Large sheep flocks, known as mobs, are found across the interiors of Queensland and New South Wales, where wells draw on artesian water. But in the harsher heat and aridity of Northern Territory and Western Australia, hardy cattle are more common. The approximate sheep–cattle boundary is marked by an amazing dingo fence that runs for 5,500km across South Australia and Queensland. The dingo is known to attack lambs but rarely calves, so the fence significantly reduces stock losses.

Within Australia's pastoral regions there are occasional 'islands' of irrigated land (these do not show up on the generalised map on page 34). The best example is the Ord River Irrigation Area, at the tropical northern tip of Western Australia, with its main crops of sugar and cotton.

RIGHT: The dingo, Australia's wild dog, poses a serious threat to grazing sheep.

ABOVE: Sheep grazing on the Darling Downs, southern Queensland.

The Murray-Darling Basin (MDB) covers an area four times larger than the UK. It has a wide network of permanent streams, plus many seasonal tributaries. Average annual rainfall ranges from 200mm in the north-west to over 1,600mm in the Snowy Mountains.

More than 85 per cent of the MDB's river water is now used. This includes transfers outside the basin to supply the population of Adelaide. To cope with increasing demand, 25 billion cubic metres of water a year are transferred into the headwaters of the Murray and Murrumbidgee rivers via the Snowy Mountains Project (see page 32). During drought periods, the Murray is often just a trickle at its mouth east of Adelaide.

Towards the north and west of the MDB, rainfall declines and the dry season extends. Farms are large and extensive sheep grazing is common. On the hills and plains of the Wimmera in western Victoria, farms average 500–800 hectares and specialise in wheat and sheep or cattle and sheep. To the north, over the Darling Downs of southern Queensland, holdings are at least 5,000 hectares and extensive sheep grazing dominates.

This trend is interrupted in two ways – firstly where rivers supply water for irrigation, and secondly where groundwater can be drawn from wells. In the MDB approximately 14,000km^2 are irrigated. The largest area is the flat Riverina region of southern New South Wales. Here, agriculture is intensive – fruit farms, vineyards and animal fattening units may be less than 200 hectares but highly productive. The upper Darling Basin, in southern Queensland, overlaps the Great Artesian Basin. Here, groundwater is pumped from wells to improve pastures for sheep.

WATER ISSUES

Concern is rising about water quantities in the MDB, because groundwater stores refill very slowly. During the twentieth century, levels in parts of the Great Artesian Basin fell by up to 120m, showing that more water was being taken out than was coming in.

Along the River Murray, water quality is a problem, too. Removal of eucalyptus woodland and scrub has caused serious salination (build-up of salts) in the soils. Pastures and crop yields are being affected and some of the salts run off into rivers. In addition, farmers have been increasing their use of chemical sprays and fertilisers. Some of these run into the rivers. The combination of natural salts and introduced chemicals is causing serious water pollution along the middle and lower Murray.

GRAZING THE OUTBACK

Across the vast, dry expanses of much of Western Australia and Northern Territory, farming means cattle ranching. Cattle stations, as the ranches are known, are huge. They average at least 50,000 hectares, with the largest over 1 million hectares. They need to be huge because the cattle have to move great distances to find grazing and water. Thus, stocking densities (the number of animals per unit area) are very low. One station in Northern Territory runs 50,000 cattle and perhaps 20,000 calves on a massive 1.25 million hectares. This is a stocking density of approximately one animal per 18 hectares.

Human population densities in the Outback, as this area is known, are very low, too. For example, in more than 1.5 million km² of northern and central Western Australia there are only 90,000 people, including 16,000 Aborigines. Settlements may be 200km apart, and the homesteads are very isolated. Many children and students learn via television, radio and computer-based programmes, or go away to boarding schools and colleges. Families rely on Flying Doctor services for medical treatment. Most homesteads house the rancher's family, with accommodation for the stockmen and their families. Many Aborigines are valuable stockmen because they understand and can tolerate the harsh environment. A single homestead may be home for up to 30 people.

The majority of the land in the Outback is still owned by the government or is under aboriginal title rights. As a result, cattle stations lease most of their land, although the long lets make it almost like ownership. An increasing amount of land is leased by large US and Asian companies.

RIGHT: Many Outback areas are so remote that light aircraft are the only practical means of transport in an emergency.
BELOW: Wooleen sheep station, Western Australia, covers more than 200,000 hectares.

CASE STUDY
THE DRYSDALE RIVER STATION
(WESTERN AUSTRALIA)

Ranchers use horses, backed up by trucks and often helicopters, to round up cattle roaming widely across the dusty red Outback terrain.

The Drysdale River cattle station covers 260,000 hectares of the rugged Kimberley Plateau in north-west Western Australia. The ranchers own the animals and machinery, but they lease the buildings and land from the government. The cattle wander across wide areas to find enough food from the sparse vegetation. During the 'Wet' – the regional name for the summer monsoon – the Drysdale River becomes a broad, shallow flood for several weeks. The water submerges all surfaced roads and the station is cut off, except by air. Cattle have to survive on pieces of higher ground. But vegetation sprouts quickly when the floods recede, providing valuable fodder for the hungry animals.

Once a year the cattle are mustered (rounded up). Helicopters are hired to help the four-wheel-drive trucks and the stockmen riding on horses. In the vast, rugged terrain, some animals may not be found – the rancher is not even sure how many cattle he has, but he estimates a total of around 7,000. Each year about 600–700 cows and bulls are sold, mostly for export as hamburger beef.

Wyndham is the nearest town, nearly 200km away, with a hospital, school and other services. Trips for supplies are made every few weeks. Homestead families are very self-reliant and may not see other people for weeks. Younger children learn at home through the School of the Air, and then go away to boarding school. The Flying Doctor comes for medical checks, but serious illness or injury means a stay in Wyndham and, for major surgery, patients need to go to Perth.

RURAL CHANGE

Since 1970, Australian agriculture has changed. The restructuring is having serious effects on rural communities. For example, numbers of farmers and farm workers fell by 16 per cent in Western Australia between 1990 and 2000. In 2001 alone, 2,000 farms closed down. By 2020, full-time farm work will probably make up less than one in four jobs in many rural districts. Farms are becoming larger but fewer, and employing fewer people. Between 1981 and 2001, 40 per cent of rural districts lost population. It is younger people who tend to move away.

CAUSES OF FARMING CHANGE

- Less protection and funding from the government.

- Increased competition in global markets.

- Changes in demand and fluctuating prices.

- Improved transport and marketing organisation.

TOWNS IN DECLINE

Agricultural and social changes affect the network of towns that grew up as service centres for rural communities. Many are losing their traditional functions and they need to adapt to survive. The combination of big-city growth, changing agriculture and rising expectations is creating major problems throughout the more remote parts of Australia. Population densities are too low to sustain services or to provide a range of career opportunities.

An increasing number of Australia's remote rural towns are in danger of decline as they lose population to the main cities.

CASE STUDY
CHANGES IN THE RURAL TOWN OF LEETON (NEW SOUTH WALES)

In the remote rural towns of Australia, most industries are closely tied to local agriculture. As agriculture changes, so must the industries, if the towns are to survive.

Leeton is a town of 6,500 people, with a surrounding rural population of 5,500. The district lies in the Murrumbidgee Irrigation Area of southern New South Wales. The main crops grown are fruits, wheat, rice and animal fodder. Leeton's industries are based on supplying the farmers and processing and distributing their products.

In 1994 the Letona Co-operative Cannery closed. This was one of the town's oldest and largest businesses, set up in 1921 and run by a co-operative of 240 local fruit growers. The main fruits canned were peaches, apricots and pears. The cannery employed up to 700 people, many seasonal. Wages to workers and payments to growers and haulage companies put more than A$20 million into the local economy each year. So the effect of the cannery's closure was, at first, serious. In 1995, 25 per cent of the shops and business premises in the main street were empty.

The chief causes of the closure were increased competition, changing tastes by consumers, insufficient funds to modernise the plant, and a reduction in government financial support.

Agriculture in the district has now adapted to changing markets – tomatoes, citrus fruits, rice and grapes are replacing the peaches and apricots. Animal feed crops are increasing to support the growing number of animal fattening enterprises. Leeton lies close to one of Australia's main wine-producing regions, so vineyards are also expanding.

Leeton is trying hard to further diversify its economy. The arrival of a company making air conditioning and hospital equipment is one example of this. Leeton lies close to the main Sydney–Melbourne road corridor, so it is well placed for transporting components and finished products. One problem Leeton faces is competition from the larger town of Griffith, located only 25km to the west, which offers a wider range of services.

LEETON'S MAIN EMPLOYERS, 1999

	EMPLOYEES	DATE ESTABLISHED
Local and state government	500	Before 1970
Cattle feedlots and abattoirs	500	Since 1990
Rice Growers Co-operative	400	Before 1970
Air conditioning & hospital equipment	120	Since 1990
Cereal and breakfast food processors	100	Since 1990
Citrus fruit processors	60	Since 1990
Engineering	50	1980s
Hay & animal feed merchants	25	1980s
Steel fabricators (farm & industrial buildings)	25	1970s

Source: *Australian Geographer*, 2000

ECONOMY AND INDUSTRY

Wool is still one of Australia's major exports, but its economic value is declining.

There was a popular saying that the Australian economy was 'carried on the back of a sheep and in a miner's barrow'. This referred to the time when the country's business was mainly in primary products – wool, meat, sugar, timber, coal and other minerals. Today, Australia's economy is much broader.

Australia is still one of the world's major sources of primary products (raw materials). But in recent years, the export of secondary (manufactured) goods has brought in more money. At the same time, the leading imports are manufactured products such as machinery, vehicles and telecommunications equipment.

ECONOMIC STRUCTURE, 2000 (% GDP CONTRIBUTIONS)

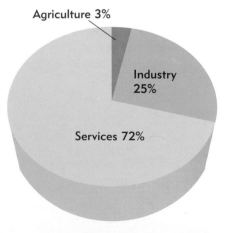

Agriculture 3%

Industry 25%

Services 72%

Source: *CIA World Factbook*, 2002

AUSTRALIA'S EXPORTS, 2001 (% OF TOTAL)

Manufacturing	45
Services	23
Mining	20
Agriculture, forestry, fishing	8
Other products	4

Source: *International Trade Statistics Yearbook*, 2002

THE JOB MARKET

The global economy prospered during much of the 1990s and this benefited Australia's industries. In 2003, there were nearly 10 million jobs and unemployment fell to just over 6 per cent (from almost 11 per cent in 1993). Figures vary from region to region. For example, in 2002 Victoria had the lowest unemployment level – 5.2 per cent – while in Tasmania about 12 per cent were without a job. More than one in five of Australia's workers are immigrants.

CHANGING TRADE

Because modern Australia developed as part of the British Empire, the UK was for a long time Australia's main trading partner. Britain's Commonwealth Preference policy meant that Australia's wool, meat and minerals had low import tariffs. However, from the 1950s, other countries became increasingly competitive. The most important change occurred when Britain joined the European Community (EC) – now the European Union (EU) – in 1973.

The Commonwealth Preference advantages were phased out during the 1960s. In response, Australia sought other markets, and looked increasingly to the USA for exports and imports. More investment came too, from US businesses such as multinational oil and mining companies. This coincided with the Australian government's move to privatise industries and reduce government subsidies.

The Sydney skyline exhibits the importance of international businesses to Australia's economy.

Since 1980, a third wave of change has seen the Australian economy forge more links with industrial east and South-east Asia. Japan is now the main trading partner and provides the leading market for Australia's coal, iron ore and pulpwood. Australia is today firmly tied to the Asian–Pacific market.

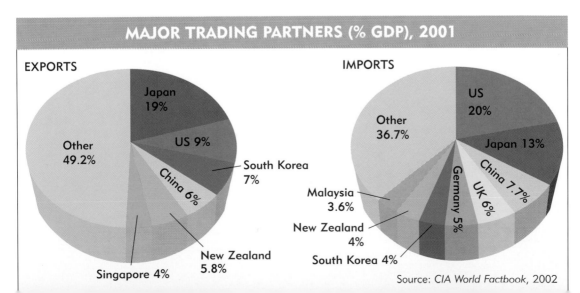

MAJOR TRADING PARTNERS (% GDP), 2001

EXPORTS

- Japan 19%
- US 9%
- South Korea 7%
- China 6%
- New Zealand 5.8%
- Singapore 4%
- Other 49.2%

IMPORTS

- US 20%
- Japan 13%
- China 7.7%
- UK 6%
- Germany 5%
- South Korea 4%
- New Zealand 4%
- Malaysia 3.6%
- Other 36.7%

Source: *CIA World Factbook*, 2002

Visitors to the Sovereign Hill Outdoor Museum in Ballarat, Victoria, can pan for gold in the reconstruction of an 1850s mining township.

MINERALS AND MINING

Australia's mineral resources have been vital to the economy for more than 150 years. Gold was discovered at Ballarat (Victoria) in 1851 and the following gold rush helped to treble Australia's population. During the twentieth century, global industrialisation boosted markets for iron ore, non-ferrous metals, fossil fuels and uranium. Growing wealth heightened demand for precious metals such as gold, and stones such as diamonds. Improved technology helped mining to grow in scale and in remoteness of location. Today Australia supplies 90 per cent of the world's opals, has the largest diamond mine and boasts the largest lead-zinc deposit.

PEAKS AND PITFALLS

Like all industries, mining is affected by world economic changes. For example, prices fell during the 1960–1990 period and Australia suffered financially. In contrast, the boom years of the 1990s saw mining grow rapidly, benefiting mineral-rich states such as Queensland and Western Australia.

One constant issue is that modern mining in remote locations is expensive and has a limited lifespan. It is also a capital-intensive industry, creating relatively few jobs compared with the amount of investment put in – fewer than 50,000 people are employed in the country's mining industry as a whole.

Mount Isa in north-west Queensland is Australia's largest underground mine and the leading world producer of silver, lead, copper and zinc.

Mining is the most important industry in Western Australia. In 2000, minerals and oil made up 70 per cent of the state's exports. One in five jobs (40,000 people) are in mining and oil. Much of the growth has been recent – in 1980 the state gold output was only 11 tonnes but by 2000 it was 250 tonnes. Mining has made Perth, the state capital, a boom city with more than 1 million inhabitants.

Western Australia's mines are widely scattered, often in remote places. The Pilbara district, 1,000km north of Perth, has the richest collection of minerals including iron ore, gold, diamonds, zinc and bauxite. They are shipped through the specialised ports of Dampier and Port Hedland. During the 1990s, a large offshore oil and gas field was developed with onshore facilities at Karratha.

GHOST TOWNS

Minerals are finite, non-renewable resources, so any individual mine has a limited lifespan despite the expense of its development. The Anaconda Nickel Corporation has recently spent A$1 billion at their new Murrin Murrin operation in the south. It will produce 45,000 tonnes of nickel and 3,000 tonnes of cobalt a year with a workforce of 600 people. But it will last only 25–30 years. Mining creates towns, such as Kalgoorlie with a population of 28,000, but they may become 'ghost towns' when mining finishes.

A specially-constructed village 8km from the Argyle diamond mine houses all workers.

FIFO

One answer to this problem in remote locations is the 'Fly-in/Fly-out' (FiFo) system. Accommodation and facilities are provided for mine workers, but not for their families. Workers 'commute' by air, usually for two-week spells at the mine. This reduces the cost of building towns that are only likely to last short-term. The remote Argyle mine in the Kimberley region is a good example. It is the world's largest diamond mine, opened in 1985, but it is expected to close in 2005. Most of the workers are flown the 1,400km from Perth, while their families remain in the city. By 2001 there were at least 50 mines operating this system, involving one-fifth of all mine workers.

WEALTH FROM MINERALS IN WESTERN AUSTRALIA, 2000

	A$ BILLION
1. Iron ore	4.2
2. Gold	3.5
3. Bauxite*	2.5
4. Nickel	1.2

*Bauxite is the ore from which aluminium is processed

Source: *Australian Geographer*, 2002

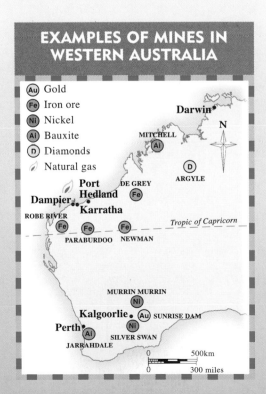

EXAMPLES OF MINES IN WESTERN AUSTRALIA

- (Au) Gold
- (Fe) Iron ore
- (Ni) Nickel
- (Al) Bauxite
- (D) Diamonds
- Natural gas

MANUFACTURING AND SERVICES

In 1970, one in four Australian workers were in the manufacturing industries. Now there are only one in eight. Because factories have become more efficient and productive, output has grown despite the decreasing workforce.

Holden cars being assembled at the Melbourne plant. The Australian Holden Company is now part of the massive US firm, General Motors.

Manufacturing industries today produce 22 per cent of the country's GDP and a substantial 45 per cent of its exports.

THRIVING OR FALLING

From the 1970s, globalisation and competition from other countries hit some of Australia's industries hard. For example, by 2001 employment in the textiles and clothing industry had dropped to less than 60,000, from almost three times that in 1971. In vehicle manufacture, the Australian Holden corporation was swallowed up by US General Motors and Japan's Mitsubishi.

CASE STUDY
MAKING KITCHEN EQUIPMENT

In 1975 there were 27 companies in Australia making refrigerators, cookers and washing machines. All were in the state capitals, except for one – the Email company – which was based in Orange, a town of 20,000 people inland from Sydney. By 1999, there were only four such companies. Email bought up businesses in Sydney, Melbourne and Adelaide and now has 60 per cent of the domestic market. It has survived competition from foreign imports by reorganising its production – a specialised factory in Orange makes refrigerators, while other products are made in Sydney and Melbourne. Email is now the largest employer in Orange, with 2,000 workers, and is the main reason why the town's population has grown to over 30,000.

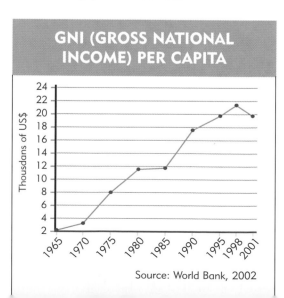

GNI (GROSS NATIONAL INCOME) PER CAPITA

Source: World Bank, 2002

Harvesting grapes for wine production, one of Australia's rapidly growing industries.

In contrast, the food and drink industries are expanding. Castlemaine and Foster's beers are sold worldwide. Since 1990, Australia's production and export of wines has doubled. The manufacture of mechanical and electronic parts is also growing, as are heavy industries such as steel works.

During the past 25 years, the following changes have occurred:

• More companies have become part of multinational corporations.
• Production has concentrated in fewer, larger, more specialised factories.
• Many companies have left core cities for the suburbs and regional towns and cities.

Between 1990 and 2000, manufacturing jobs in Sydney and Melbourne declined by 10 per cent. But in the outer suburbs and regional towns, they grew by more than 15 per cent. Newcastle and Wollongong, to either side of Sydney, are important centres for metals and machinery. Vehicle assembly plants and component suppliers cluster outside Melbourne. Around 70 per cent of all Australia's manufacturing jobs are in the Sydney–Melbourne region.

THE SERVICES REVOLUTION

Over the past 30 years, the rapid growth of service industries has changed the structure of Australia's economy. These industries now provide 63 per cent of the country's GDP, up from 52 per cent in 1980. Three in every four jobs fall within the services category.

• 37 per cent of service sector employees have professional, administrative, managerial and technical jobs.
• Between 1985 and 2002, jobs in financial, property and business services doubled to almost 1.4 million.
• During the 1990s, jobs in service industries grew by an average of 19 per cent a year, compared with 4 per cent in other industries.
• 'Knowledge-based' industries, such as financial services, computer programming and legal services, have provided half of all jobs created since 1970, and they now generate 50 per cent of GDP.
• The Australian film and television industry is now a major global competitor.
• Service industries provide increasing job opportunities for women.

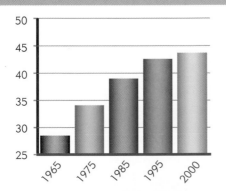

FEMALE LABOUR FORCE (% OF TOTAL)

Source: Social Watch, 2003

ENERGY AND FUEL PRODUCTION

Australia used twice as much energy in 2001 as it did in 1971. This was due to a combination of population growth, economic expansion and rising standards of living – electricity demand rose by 65 per cent between 1981 and 2001. New South Wales and Victoria are responsible for almost 60 per cent of the country's energy consumption.

More than 90 per cent of Australia's energy comes from fossil fuels. This is not surprising considering the country's rich mineral fuel resources – only oil needs to be imported. Almost two-thirds of all electricity is generated by coal-fired power stations. Yet, over half of the coal mined is exported. The recent exploitation of large natural gas fields off the coast of Western Australia explains why production of this fuel has rocketed.

COAL

Australia is a major producer and the world's leading exporter of coal. In 2001, out of an output of 335 million tonnes, 194 million tonnes were exported. The main coalfields are close to the coast, so they are convenient for shipping to international markets.

ENERGY PRODUCTION, 2001

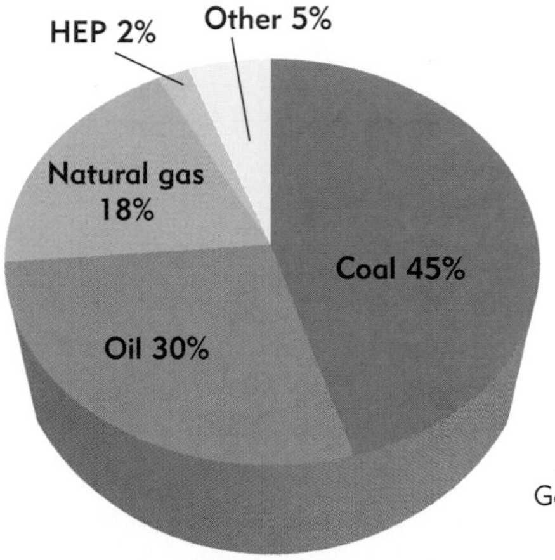

HEP 2% Other 5%
Natural gas 18%
Coal 45%
Oil 30%

Source: Australian Government Website

An aerial view of the coal terminal at Newcastle, just north of Sydney on the coast of New South Wales. Coal is delivered here from inland mines and loaded onto ships for export.

FOSSIL FUELS OUTPUT, 1991 & 2001

	1991	2001
Coal (million tonnes)	250	335
Oil (million m^3)	32	37
Gas (1,000 tonnes)	331	914

Source: *World Development Reports*, 1992, 2001

Because Australia relies on fossil fuels for energy and export, the Australian government was reluctant to sign the 1991 Kyoto Treaty on reducing atmospheric pollution. Australia has one of the world's highest emission rates per head of population. The target of the 1991 Treaty was to reduce emissions by at least 8 per cent by 2010. Between 1991 and 2001, emissions in Australia *increased* by 13 per cent.

TRAFFIC AND TRANSPORT

Australian transport is dominated by two factors – the huge size of the country and the clustered population. In the cities, there are more than 12 million motor vehicles for fewer than 20 million people. Traffic densities and commuter surges are similar to those in the UK and there are enough people to support public transport systems. However, when you drive beyond the cities, the lack of traffic is striking. Much of Australia is very empty and has few surfaced roads. There may be 400km between petrol stations or settlements. You will cover 14,900km if you drive around Australia on the main highway – without even going to Tasmania! It is very expensive to maintain the 330,000km of surfaced road.

A rail network along the east coast and west–east links Melbourne, Adelaide and Perth. In 2002, a south–north line between Adelaide and Darwin was completed. Railways are efficient for freight but too slow for most people – it takes a train two days to get from Perth to Adelaide, for example. Air travel is the obvious way to overcome distances – you can fly from Perth to Sydney in five hours – but there are too few passengers to keep fares low. The government has reduced its funding and internal airlines find it difficult to survive. The hope is that as international tourism and Australia's population continue to grow, passenger volumes will increase. Meanwhile, telecommunications remains a vital industry.

TELECOMMUNICATIONS DATA, 2001

Mainline Phones	10,050,000
Mobile Phones	8,600,000
Internet Service Providers	603

CIA World Factbook, 2002

A 'road train' rolls along the lonely Victoria Highway in a remote part of Western Australia.

CONSERVATION, LEISURE AND TOURISM

Salt-ravaged agricultural land in the Wimmera District, north-west Victoria.

Australians are very proud of their country. They love their unique environment but are increasingly aware of how they are affecting it. Conservation has become an important issue, with the aim of reducing the damage caused by industry, agriculture and, increasingly, leisure and tourism.

IMPACTS OF AGRICULTURE

A recent survey estimated that 50 per cent of pasture and 30 per cent of arable land showed noticeable signs of degradation – in other words, it was becoming less productive. Sheep and cattle grazing, even in low numbers, can quickly reduce the sparse vegetation of arid areas. This leads to erosion of the soil and further loss of vegetation.

SOME ENVIRONMENTAL THREATS

- Urban sprawl
- Intensification of agriculture
- Deforestation
- Increasing demands for minerals and water
- Introduced species
- Growth of leisure and tourism

In more intensely farmed, moister regions, soil salination has become a major problem. The main cause is the clearance of woodland, whose vegetation would normally maintain the balance of salts in the soils. Without the trees, natural salts build up to unusually high levels. This leads to poor plant growth and crop failure. Some of the salts are also flushed into streams, which then contaminate urban water supplies and irrigation systems. State governments are encouraging reforestation projects to reduce the threat of salination.

IMPACTS OF FORESTRY

Dense forests in Australia are limited to the upland fringes and Tasmania. For many years, logging companies have exploited these valuable resources – one-third of the old-growth forests have been cleared or disturbed. Over the past 30 years, environmental groups and government agencies have campaigned against this. In Queensland, logging of the tropical rainforests is now severely controlled, but this has meant loss of jobs and income.

ABOVE: Logs from a regrowth forest in the Styx Valley, southern Tasmania, are tied down for transport to a pulp and paper mill.
LEFT: The destruction of eucalyptus forests poses a serious threat to the koala which depends on eucalyptus leaves for food and moisture.

Western Tasmania is a magnificent landscape of forested mountains and deep river valleys. For several decades, environmental groups have fought to conserve this natural beauty. In the 1980s they prevented the building of a large dam and reservoir for HEP in the spectacular gorge of the Franklin River. Several national parks have been combined into the high-conservation Tasmania Wilderness World Heritage Area (TWWHA). But despite this, large-scale logging continues.

CONSERVATION OR ECONOMY?

Tasmania is the world's second-largest exporter of woodchips, after the USA. At present almost all of the output comes from old-growth forests. These precious temperate rainforests have more species of plants and animals than any other ecosystem in Australia. Yet in 2003, despite some protection within the TWWHA, an area the size of 15 football pitches was being cleared each day. The logging and woodchip industry is important to the state economy. It employs over 5,000 people and demand is growing. In recent years, Tasmania's unemployment rate has hovered around 12 per cent, and young people have left for Melbourne and Sydney. If logging is reduced, unemployment will rise. There is debate over which is more important – conservation of the island, or its economy.

THREATS TO NATIVE SPECIES

The spread of farming and forestry has ruined habitats for many native creatures – the koala, for example, eats only eucalyptus foliage, so woodland clearance is fatal. The introduction of new species, intentionally and by accident, is another serious problem. All major farm animals and crops have been brought from other continents. There are also domestic and wild creatures – horses, cats, dogs, foxes and rabbits – all from Europe. Because many of Australia's species – such as koalas, wombats and echidnas (spiny anteaters) – have not developed ways of defending themselves from introduced species, they are easy targets for foxes and wild (feral) cats. In turn, because of the good food supply, the intruder species have thrived and multiplied. Today, one of the main aims in national parks and other protected reserves is to remove all introduced species and provide safe habitats for native species.

ANIMAL PLAGUES

Rabbits are hardy animals that breed rapidly and destroy grazing pastures. Since arriving in Australia, their population has exploded to hundreds of millions and the government has declared them a national plague. Attempts to control numbers include shooting, poisoning and rabbit-proof fencing such as the 2,000km fence across Western Australia.

The impacts of introduced species continue. In the 1930s, cane toads were introduced to control an insect that was attacking Queensland's sugar cane plants. Unfortunately, the project failed. The toads have since multiplied dramatically and become a widespread pest, harming native ecosystems and even injuring humans with their poisonous bite.

BELOW: Rabbit 'plagues' devastate grazing land.
MAIN PICTURE: Victoria's Grampians National Park is a protected area of great natural beauty.

AUSTRALIANS AT PLAY

Outdoor recreation on land and in water plays an important part in Australian culture. For a country with fewer than 20 million people, Australia has impressive large-scale sporting achievements. It is a world leader in cricket, rugby, tennis, sailing, surfing and swimming and has many top quality facilities, including the National Sports Academy. The success of the 2000 Olympic Games in Sydney illustrates the country's sporting pride and enthusiasm.

A favourable climate and spacious suburban homes encourage outdoor 'barbie and beer' lifestyles. Most of Australia's population live within 20km of the coast, so beaches and water sports – such as surfing, windsurfing and sailing – are very popular. The annual Sydney–Hobart yacht race is a leading world event. More than 30 per cent of people take part in some form of water-based activity.

On land, hiking or 'bush-bashing' is popular. All states have national parks – with camping facilities, trails and wilderness areas – and these attract more than 5 million people a year. Some, such as the Royal Sydney National Park,

are close to cities. Others can be reached for weekend breaks, for example Wilson's Promontory National Park – a three hour drive from Melbourne. Some, such as the Kakadu National Park in Northern Territory, are far more remote and require long-distance travel.

Recently, the development of four-wheel-drive vehicles and high-tech camping equipment has encouraged more Australians to explore remote parts of their country. For example, in 1980 there were fewer than 20,000 visitors to Queensland's Fraser Island. Today, more than 250,000 people flock there per year, since the upgrading of ferry facilities and the introduction of off-road vehicles.

People are becoming more concerned about the impact that this growth in outdoor recreation will have on the environment.

Queensland's Fraser Island can be explored by off-road vehicle, but access areas are restricted to protect threatened habitats and species.

Along the coasts, there are strong planning controls because of pressures to build more marinas and develop more beaches. To help protect the fragile Fraser Island environment, a zoning plan has been introduced, restricting the use of off-road vehicles to certain areas. Many other national parks have similar zoning policies. In Wilson's Promontory National Park, all major camping facilities are concentrated in one location. Elsewhere in the park there are no surfaced roads and only 'primitive' small-scale campsites. The aim is to protect the delicate habitats and endangered species such as koalas and wombats.

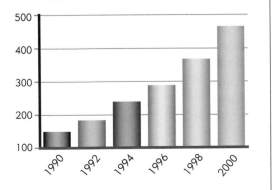

PERSONAL COMPUTERS PER 1,000 PEOPLE

Sources: World Development Indicators, World Bank

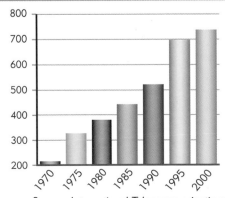

TELEVISION SETS PER 1,000 PEOPLE

Source: International Telecommunications Union

Adventurous tourists are increasingly attracted by exploration into remote Outback areas such as this bush camp in South Australia.

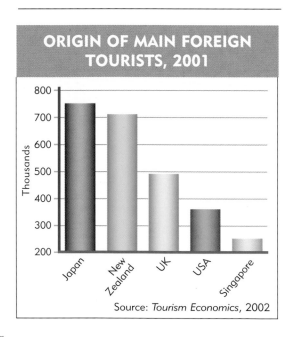

ORIGIN OF MAIN FOREIGN TOURISTS, 2001

Thousands

800
700
600
500
400
300
200

Japan | New Zealand | UK | USA | Singapore

Source: *Tourism Economics*, 2002

TOURISM: A BOOM INDUSTRY

Australia is becoming increasingly popular as a tourist destination. In 2001 there were approximately 5 million visitors to Australia, bringing in A$17 billion – over 4 per cent of GDP. More than a third of Australia's tourists come from Asia, especially Japan. The large numbers from New Zealand show the close connections between the two countries.

REASONS FOR TOURISM

The majority of Australia's visitors are holidaymakers, and a further fifth are visiting friends and relatives. This is not surprising when you think how many immigrants live in Australia (see page 22). New South Wales attracts 40 per cent of all foreign visitors, with Sydney the main centre. Queensland, with its alluring environment, glorious coastline and

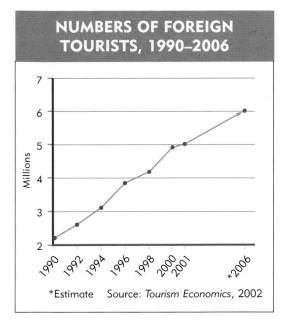

NUMBERS OF FOREIGN TOURISTS, 1990–2006

*Estimate   Source: *Tourism Economics*, 2002

in luxury beach resorts; there are specialist wildlife trips and large-scale package tours. Australia is popular with gap year students, who often go backpacking for several months, staying in hostels and finding temporary jobs. At the other extreme, most Japanese tourists travel on mass package tours, making brief visits to a small number of famous places.

DOMESTIC TOURISM

Australians take at least 70 million business and pleasure trips a year within their own country. Most business travellers fly between the big cities. Seaside areas, especially Queensland's Gold Coast and the Great Barrier Reef, are the most popular holiday destinations. Coastal and mountain districts within weekend reach of the big cities are also growing rapidly. South of Perth in Western Australia, the population of the Cape Naturaliste to Cape Leeuwin area has recently increased by 50 per cent. In 2000, tourism projects worth A$80 million were under construction there, including holiday homes for Perth families.

the Great Barrier Reef, gets 25 per cent of all 'visitor nights' (one visitor night = one person staying for one night).

Tourists are drawn by Australia's superb variety, both in nature and in culture. There are adventure treks to the Outback and stays

CASE STUDY
TOURISM COMES TO CAIRNS

In 1976, Cairns, on the coast of northern Queensland, had a population of 57,000 and its economy was based on agriculture. A small number of tourists travelled there, mainly by boat. In 2002, the population had more than doubled – largely due to a tourism boom. Today, a third of all foreign visitors to Australia include Cairns on their itinerary. The prime attractions are the Great Barrier Reef (see pages 56–57) and the wildlife-rich tropical rainforests.

Cairns and its neighbouring coastline have 10,000 hotel rooms, 3,000 holiday

rental flats, 3,000 beds in hostels and sites for 7,500 caravans. Yearly, around 500,000 international visitors and 400,000 Australians stay an average of six nights in the region. Vital elements in this expansion have been:
• The opening of Cairns International Airport to take wide-bodied jets (1983).
• The introduction of high-speed catamarans, allowing day-trips to the Great Barrier Reef (early 1980s).
• The use of four-wheel-drive vehicles to make tracks into the rainforests (1990s).
• The encouragement of foreign investment (for example, 40 per cent of investment since 1980 has been from Japan and South-east Asia).

TOURISM AND THE GREAT BARRIER REEF

The Great Barrier Reef is the world's largest coral reef system and perhaps Australia's most famous natural attraction. It runs for 2,000km off the east coast of Queensland and has 3,000 separate reefs, islands and cays. In total, it covers an area greater than the states of Tasmania and Victoria combined.

THE RICHNESS OF THE REEF

A coral is a plant-like animal that lives in close combination with certain types of algae. As the corals die, their skeletons gradually make up a limestone platform on which the colourful living coral sits. The Great Barrier Reef has built up slowly over 10,000 years. It is the most diverse and productive ecosystem in the world. There are 400 types of coral, 1,500 species of fish, 4,000 types of mollusc and six of the seven known species of turtle. In every hectare of water there may be 100,000 fish.

THE SENSITIVE REEF

Corals need the sea water to be at least 18°C, and clear so that sunlight can penetrate. The algae on which the corals depend need sunlight to photosynthesise food. So living coral is generally found in shallow water, less than 20m deep. Like the corals themselves, many species that live on the reef are highly specialised. They need constant conditions in order to survive and are very sensitive to changes in the reef environment.

THREATS TO THE REEF

The reef is very attractive, especially for commercial fishing and tourism. In 2002, tourism brought some A$4 billion to Queensland's economy. In 1990 the reef received 2.5 million tourists and by 2000 this had grown to 4 million, 60 per cent of whom were foreign visitors. Most visitors are on day-trips from harbours such as Cairns and Port Douglas. They fish, snorkel, scuba-dive or observe from glass-bottomed boats. Increasing numbers of islands have luxury resorts, marinas and even airstrips. The continuing pressure to bring in more tourists is just one of the serious threats to the fragile reef.

The colourful reef, teeming with marine life, is a great attraction for divers. It is a rich but fragile ecosystem.

MAIN THREATS TO THE REEF

- Pollution from boats, growing coastal towns and agricultural chemicals.
- Silt from local deforestation and mangrove clearance, making the water cloudy.
- Direct impacts by increasing numbers of tourists and boats.
- Growing pressures from commercial and recreational fishing.
- Intrusive species such as the 'crown of thorns' starfish which eat the live coral, preventing regrowth (during the 1980s a population explosion of this species caused extensive coral damage).
- Global warming (and hence rising water temperatures) which causes coral bleaching as individual corals die away (in 2002, 60 per cent of the reef area showed some bleaching damage).

MANAGING THE REEF

The reef now lies within the Great Barrier Reef Marine Park (GBRMP). The park's aim is '*to provide for the protection, wise use, understanding and enjoyment of the Great Barrier Reef in perpetuity*'. This gives managers the difficult task of balancing vital conservation measures with optimum use of the park.

The park plan is based on a zoning system that controls the way each area is used. For example, all commercial businesses must have a licence, which is hard to get. This allows them to operate in certain zones, but limits what they can do and when and where they can go. To protect the most precious and fragile areas, a series of 'green zones' excludes tourists and fishing boats from

almost 5 per cent of the park. In 2003 the managers introduced a plan to extend these conservation zones to 30 per cent of the park.

AUSTRALIA'S FUTURE

The Great Barrier Reef sums up some key questions facing Australians about their future: how to use their resources and how to conserve them. They are proud of their young country and its wonderful environment. At the same time they are increasingly aware of both the benefits and the threats of increasing populations and continued economic expansion. They want their population and economy to grow, but they are concerned about losing control of this growth. For example, how can they reap the benefits of the developing markets of eastern Asia without being swamped by them? The government faces challenging times, but the potential rewards for Australia are great.

Heron Island is one of three coral cays on the Great Barrier Reef that have tourist facilities. It is world famous for turtle breeding.

GLOSSARY

Aquifer A layer of underground rock that soaks up and stores water.

Arid A term used to describe an environment that generally receives less than 250mm annual rainfall.

Birth rate The number of children born in a year per 1,000 population.

Boom city A city that experiences rapid economic growth.

Cay A small, flat sand island overlying a coral reef.

Colony (political) A territory that is taken over and ruled by another country.

Counterurbanisation The movement of people from cities to live in smaller towns and rural settlements.

Depression A low-pressure atmospheric system.

Dingo The wild dog of Australia.

Diversification Broadening an economy or business by adding new activities.

Drainage basin The total area that contributes water to a river.

Ecosystem A system that represents the relationships within a community of living things (plants and animals) and between this community and their non-living environment. An ecosystem can be as small as a pond or as large as the Earth.

Emigration The movement of people away from a country, city, or other place, to live elsewhere.

Erosion The wearing away of soil or rock by the forces of nature (such as wind and rain) or the actions of people (such as deforestation).

Estuary The mouth of a river where it broadens into the sea.

Federation A country that is divided into regions (states) whose individual governments take greater control of their own affairs with a lesser role for the central government.

Fertility rate The average number of children a woman gives birth to during her lifetime.

Flash flood A sudden flood in a dry stream bed, caused by a heavy rainstorm.

Fodder crop A crop grown to be fed to animals.

GDP (Gross Domestic Product) The monetary value of goods and services produced by a country in a single year.

Gentrification The process by which older, run-down urban neighbourhoods are improved by relatively affluent people moving in.

Glacial trough A deep valley, often U-shaped, carved by a glacier.

Globalisation When large corporations base themselves in a number of different countries.

GNI (Gross National Income) Sometimes called Gross National Product or GNP, this is the monetary value of goods and services produced by a country, plus any earnings from overseas, in a single year.

Homeland The traditional territory of an indigenous group of people.

HEP (Hydroelectric power) Electricity generated by water as it passes through turbines.

Immigration The movement of people into a country, city, or other place, to live.

Intensification Farming more intensively to increase productivity per unit area of land.

Irrigation The controlled addition of water to agricultural land to improve plant growth.

Marsupial A type of mammal whose females use a pouch to carry their immature young.

Monsoon The seasonal period of heavy rains, or the heavy rains themselves, experienced in a tropical climate.

Mortality rate The number of people who die in a year per 1,000 population.

Mulla mulla A wild, flowering shrub native to parts of Australia.

Multinational corporation A large business that has operations in a number of countries.

Natural increase The excess of births over deaths.

Old-growth forest An original forest, before any logging or replanting has taken place.

Outback A general term for the remote, sparsely populated interior regions of Australia.

Photosynthesis The process by which plants use sunlight to make energy-rich food from carbon dioxide and water, releasing oxygen.

Plateau A relatively flat-topped upland landform.

Population structure The numbers and proportion of people in particular age-groups within a given population.

Productivity The output achieved from a certain level of resource use, investment and effort.

Quota A form of control or rationing that states a limit, for example the amount of wheat a farm may produce in a year.

Refugee A migrant who has been forced to flee from his/her country.

Regeneration The revival of a declining area.

Salination An unhealthy build-up of natural salts in the surface of the soil.

Savannah A dryland ecosystem dominated by grassland with scattered trees and bushes.

Semi-arid A term used to describe an environment that generally receives 250–400mm annual rainfall.

Specialisation The concentration on one or a small number of products or services.

Subsidy A contribution of money, especially one made by a government to support a project.

Tablelands Relatively flat-topped uplands, usually edged with steep, descending slopes.

Tariff A tax on imports, intended to protect local products.

Temperate Usually refers to climates without great extremes of heat or cold.

FURTHER INFORMATION

BOOKS TO READ:

Eyewitness Travel Guides: Australia (Dorling Kindersley Publishing, 2003) Illustrated reference.

Fodor's Explore Australia 2003 (Random House Inc, 2004). Comprehensive illustrated guidebook.

Lonely Planet Australia by Paul Harding (Editor), 11th Edition (Lonely Planet Publications, 2002) Comprehensive illustrated travel guidebook.

Lizard Island: Science and Scientists on Australia's Great Barrier Reef by Sneed B., III Collard (Franklin Watts Books, 2000) A narrative study of marine life on the Great Barrier Reef, set at Lizard Island Research Station.

The National Geographic Traveler: Australia by Roff Martin-Smith (AA Publishing, 1999) A comprehensive guidebook with visitor tips, maps and environmental and historical information.

The Rough Guide to Australia (Rough Guides, 2003) Comprehensive travel guidebook.

WEBSITES:

GENERAL INFORMATION ON AUSTRALIA:

www.csu.edu.au/australia
www.odci.gov/cia/publications/factbook/geos/as.html
www.australiangeographic.com/index.cfm
www.gov.au (Government website)
www.dfat.gov.au/geo/australia (Factsheets)
www.abs.gov.au (Statistics)
www.dpie.gov.au (Agriculture)
www.erin.gov.au (Environment)

ABORIGINAL CULTURE:

www.aboriginalaustralia.com
www.aboriginalart.com.au
www.nlc.org.au

TOURIST INFORMATION:

www.australia.com
www.atn.com.au
www.about-australia.com
www.greatbarrierreef.aus.net

FILM:

Rabbit Proof Fence Directed by Philip Noyce (Rated PG, released 2002; available on video and DVD, 2003) Based on the true story of three aboriginal girls and their struggle for freedom in 1930s Australia.

JOURNALS:

Australian Geographer (Journal of the Geographical Society of New South Wales, published quarterly)

Australian Geographical Studies (Journal of the Institute of Australian Geographers, also quarterly)

USEFUL ADDRESS:

Australian High Commission
Australia House
The Strand
London WC28 4LA

INDEX

Numbers shown in **bold** refer to pages with maps, graphic illustrations or photographs.

A shingleback or stumpy-tailed lizard, one of Australia's unique reptile species.

Pink mulla mullas and snappy gums at the Millstream-Chichester National Park in Pilbarra, Western Australia.